OUTBACK BABIES

KANGAROO JOEYS

by Genevieve Nilsen

TABLE OF CONTENTS

tadpole books

WORDS TO KNOW

boxes

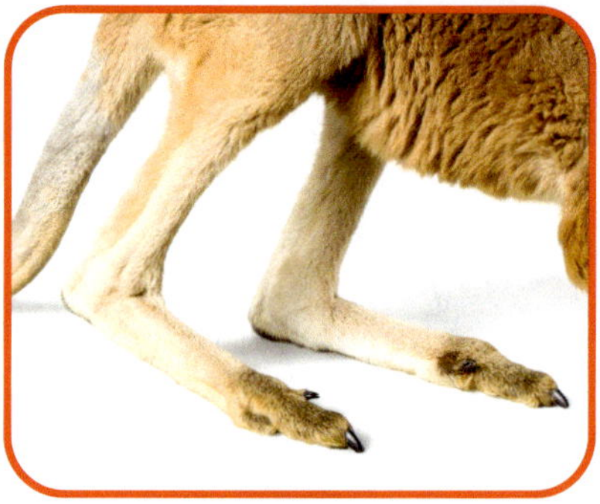

feet

hops

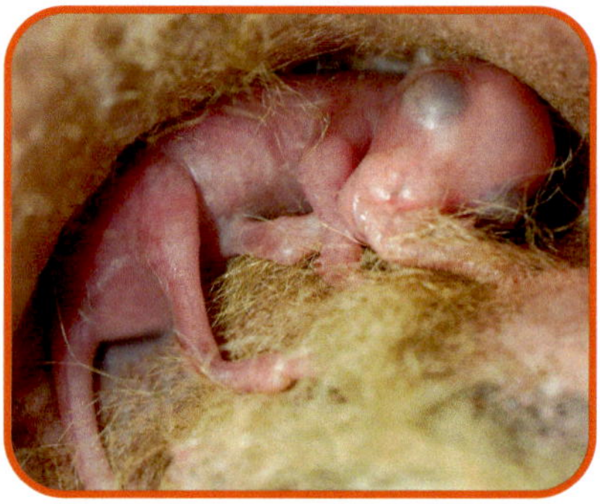

joey

pouch

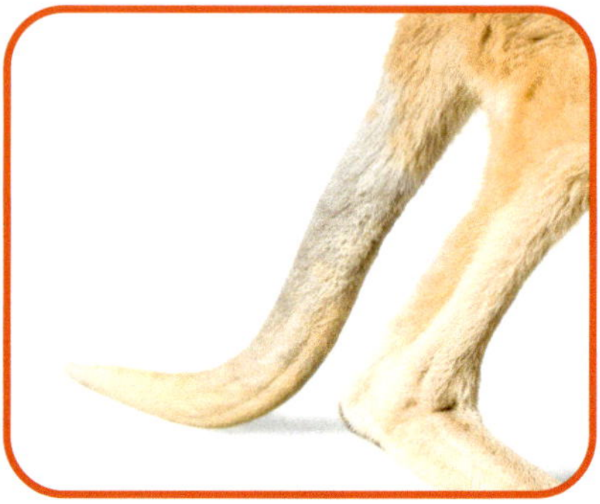

tail

KANGAROO JOEYS

This mom has a pouch!

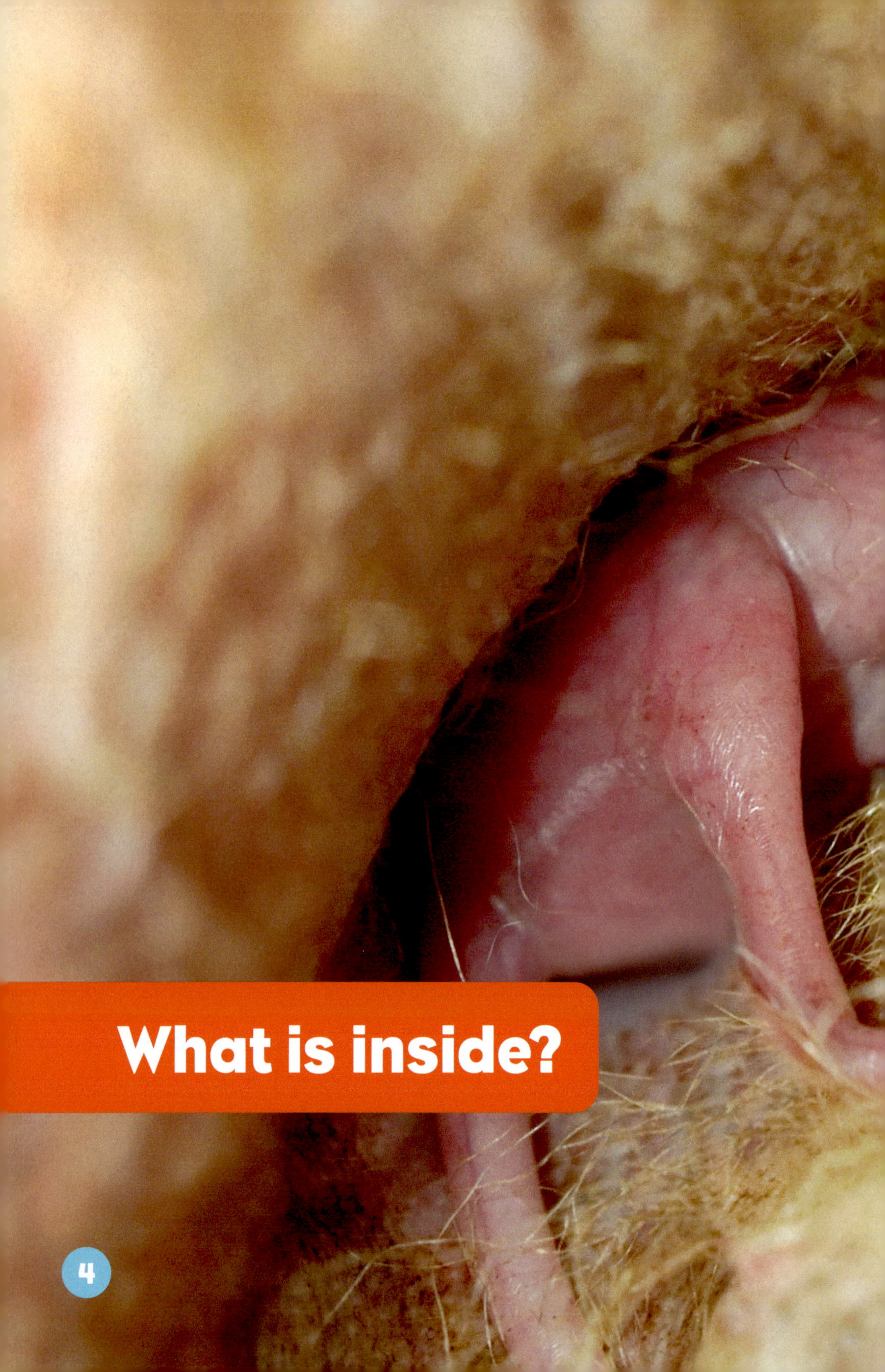

What is inside?

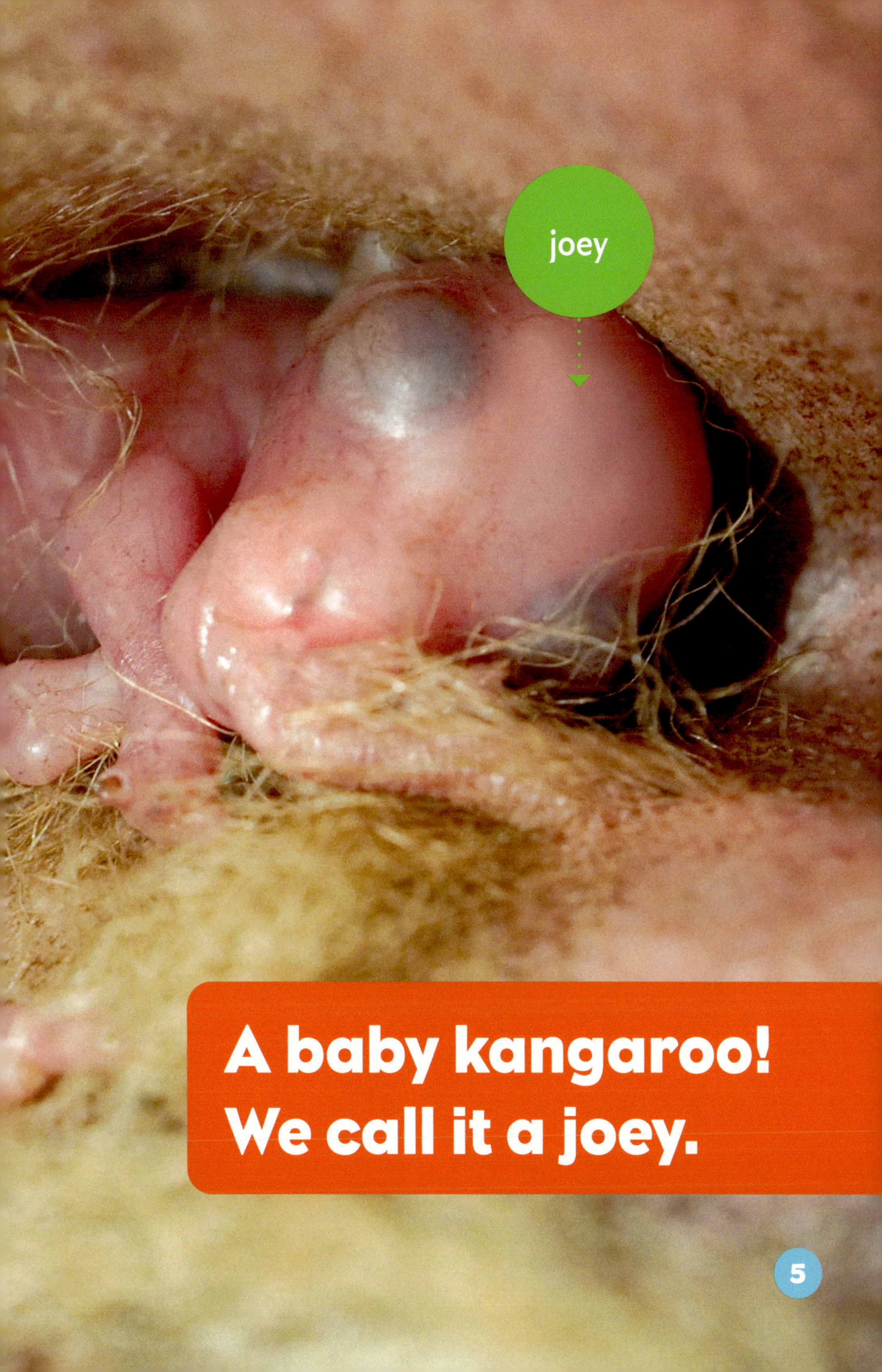

A baby kangaroo! We call it a joey.

pouch

It stays in the pouch.

The joey grows.

He leaves the pouch!

He hops.

Big feet help.

A long tail helps, too.

The joey grows up.

He boxes!

LET'S REVIEW!

What is this kangaroo joey doing?

INDEX